To Chase
from Mrs. Cieply,
Agora Family Coach :)
3/2/18

Meet my neighbor, the
hip-hop dancer

Marc Crabtree
Author and Photographer

🌱 **Crabtree Publishing Company**

www.crabtreebooks.com

♣ Crabtree Publishing Company

Meet my Neighbor

Meet my neighbor, the hip-hop dancer

Dedicated by Marcelino DaCosta:
For The DaCosta & Greaves Family, Ground illusionz, Conscious Soles,
C.F.M., U.N.I.T.Y., R.H.Y.T.H.M., Mississauga Arts Council, 1 Unit Tribe,
BluePrint For Life, and finally to my mentors and students.

Author and photographer
Marc Crabtree

Editorial director
Kathy Middleton

Editor
Reagan Miller

Proofreader
Crystal Sikkens

Design and prepress technician
Samantha Crabtree

Production coordinator
Margaret Amy Salter

Print coordinator
Katherine Berti

Photographs
All photographs by Marc Crabtree except:
Kerrie Chen: front cover
Shutterstock: pages 3, 24 (turntables)

Library and Archives Canada Cataloguing in Publication

Crabtree, Marc
 Meet my neighbor, the hip-hop dancer / Marc Crabtree.

(Meet my neighbor)
Issued also in electronic formats.
ISBN 978-0-7787-4558-7 (bound).--ISBN 978-0-7787-4563-1 (pbk.)

 1. DaCosta, Marcelino--Juvenile literature. 2. Dancers--Canada--
Biography--Juvenile literature. 3. Hip-hop dance--Juvenile
literature. I. Title. II. Series: Crabtree, Marc. Meet my neighbor.

GV1785.D22C73 2012   j792.802'8092   C2011-907923-2

Library of Congress Cataloging-in-Publication Data

Crabtree, Marc.
Meet my neighbor, the hip-hop dancer / Marc Crabtree.
p. cm. -- (Meet my neighbor)
Includes index.
ISBN 978-0-7787-4558-7 (reinforced library binding : alk. paper) --
ISBN 978-0-7787-4563-1 (pbk. : alk. paper) -- ISBN 978-1-4271-7896-1
(electronic pdf) -- ISBN 978-1-4271-8011-7 (electronic html)
1. Hip-hop dance--Juvenile literature. I. Title.

GV1796.H57C73 2012
793.3--dc23

2011047836

Crabtree Publishing Company

www.crabtreebooks.com   1-800-387-7650

Printed in Canada/012012/MA20111130

Published in Canada
Crabtree Publishing
616 Welland Ave.
St. Catharines, Ontario
L2M 5V6

Published in the United States
Crabtree Publishing
PMB 59051
350 Fifth Avenue, 59th Floor
New York, New York 10118

Published in the United Kingdom
Crabtree Publishing
Maritime House
Basin Road North, Hove
BN41 1WR

Published in Australia
Crabtree Publishing
3 Charles Street
Coburg North
VIC 3058

Contents

Meet my Neighbor

Meet my neighbors, Marcelino DaCosta, and his family. Marcelino is a hip-hop dancer.

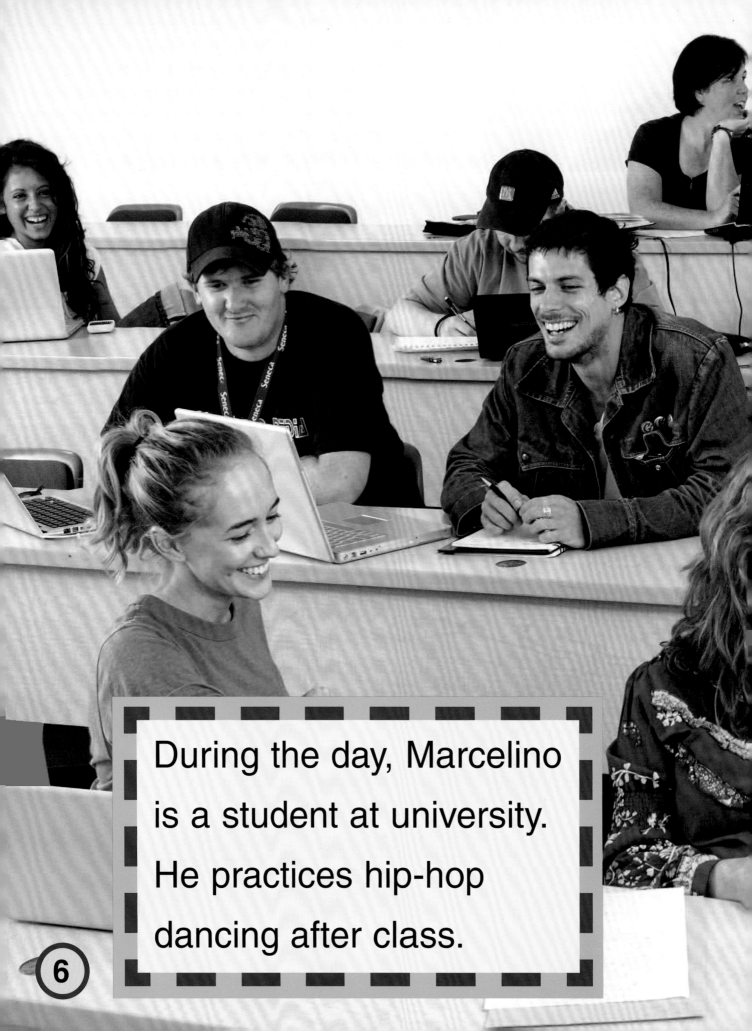

During the day, Marcelino is a student at university. He practices hip-hop dancing after class.

7

Hip-hop dancers move to hip-hop music. Hip-hop music is a mix of rap and fast beats.

Marcelino has been a hip-hop dancer for many years. He also teaches hip-hop dancing to others.

Marcelino and his **dance crew** practice their dance moves.

A dance crew is a group of dancers who perform together.

11

Marcelino's dance crew joins in a **dance battle**. A dance battle is a contest between two dance crews. The dance crews perform for judges. The judges decide which dance crew is the best.

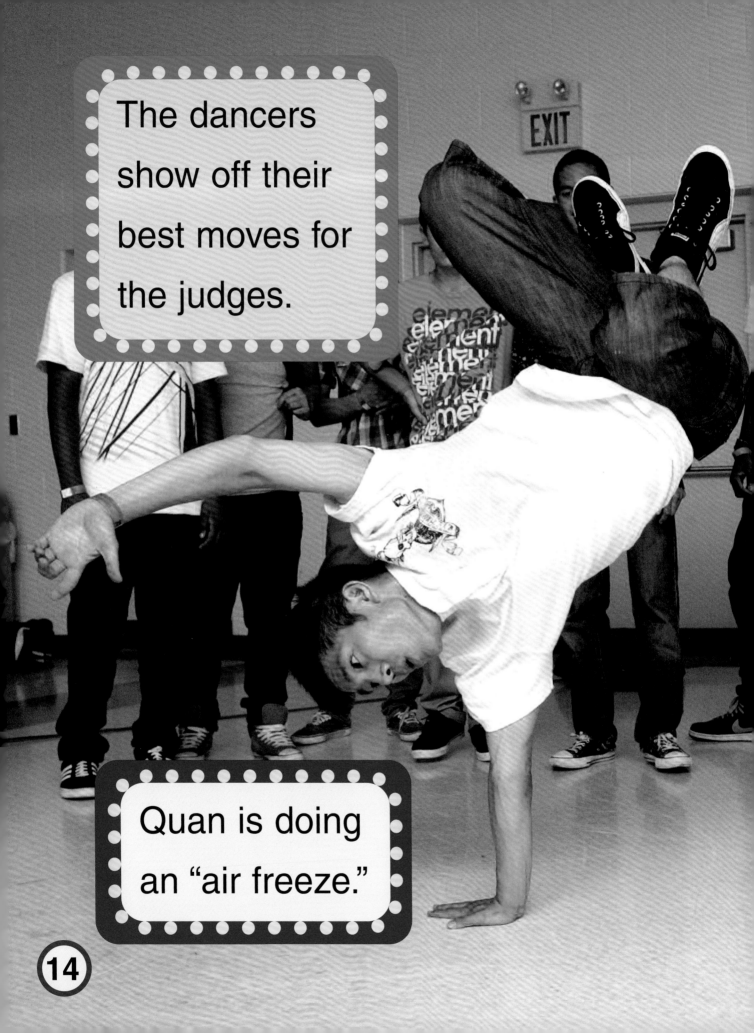

The dancers show off their best moves for the judges.

Quan is doing an "air freeze."

Louie is doing a "head spin."

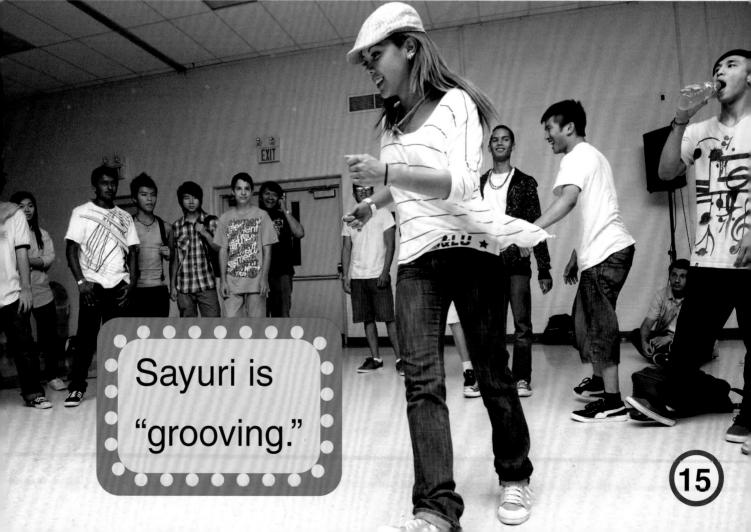

Sayuri is "grooving."

Marcelino shows off his "footwork."

Adrian is spinning a "windmill."

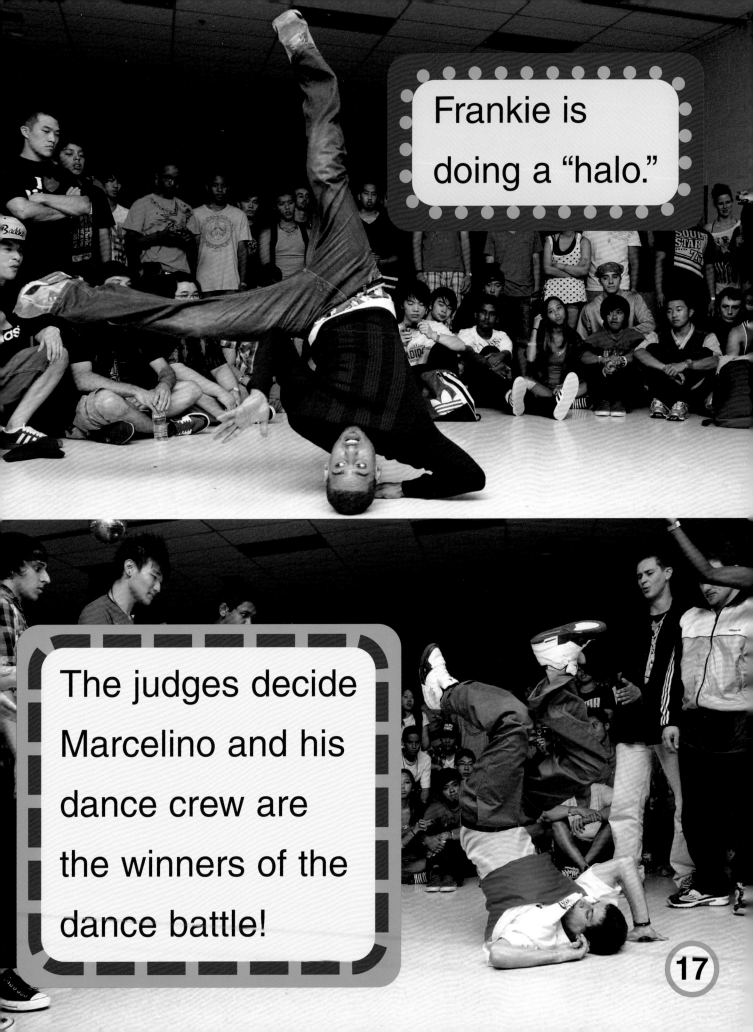

Frankie is doing a "halo."

The judges decide Marcelino and his dance crew are the winners of the dance battle!

Rapping and **DJing** are also part of the hip-hop culture.

Culture is a way of life or shared interests that bring a group of people together. A rapper writes rhymes or poems. He or she raps, or speaks, the rhymes along with the DJ's beats.

A DJ uses **turntables** and other equipment to create the beats.

Graffiti art is also an important part of hip-hop culture.

Graffiti artists use spray paint to create their colorful designs. Artists must get permission from the owner of the building before they paint on its walls.

Last year, Marcelino traveled to the Arctic to teach these children about hip-hop dance and culture.

Glossary

dance battle

dance crew

DJing

graffiti

rapping

turntables